ISBN 978-0-915545-13-1
First Printing 2013

Published by
Stanley R. Abbott Ministries, Inc.
P.O. Box 533
McRae, Georgia 31055
U.S.A.

THE RIDDLE

PREFACE

Dictionary.com defines *"...riddle..."* as a puzzling question, problem, or matter. While God has designed *"...simplicity..."* as a way of life in Christ, the enemy through his subtle craftiness is always seeking to corrupt the way of God. Life involving repentance, forgiveness, and restoration of relationship where sin has been committed is just such a place in which the enemy's corruption has eroded the truth for generations. Today repentance has been reduced to, *"Sorry about that..."*, or some similarly glib saying. Forgiveness has been diminished to little more than, *"Oh, it's okay..."*.

I remember seeing a minister on television actually bring a repentant brother who had sinned onto camera, receive the sinning brother's repentance, and then offer forgiveness to the brother while praying over the situation. The television minister's actions sent a reverberation through the church in North America that seemed to reach every born again person in every local assembly. The general consensus was, *"Wow, we have never seen anything like that. Awesome!"*

How could something so fundamental to life in Christ have been *"...new..."* to ministers and believers alike all across the nation? The answer is very profound: It is because the enemy's subtle craftiness has made the concept of sin, repentance, and forgiveness a *"...riddle..."*! Instead of being a simple fundamental by which the church lives, sin, repentance, and forgiveness have become puzzling questions, problems, or matters void of most real practical meaning to the church. We must unravel the riddle to make dealing with sin, repentance, and forgiveness fundamental to our life in Christ once again!

THE RIDDLE

Table of Contents

THE RIDDLE

Chapter One

THE ENTRANCE OF SIN & DEATH

God gave Adam responsibility and authority to rule over all the works of God's hands at the time of creation. This appointment for Adam to rule was contingent upon Adam's continued submission to his Creator. The moment Adam yielded to an authority who was not his Creator, three immediate consequences resulted:

> ➤ *Adam was separated from his Creator;*

> ➤ *Authority to rule over all the works of God's hands "...transferred..." from Adam to the one in authority to whom Adam yielded;*

> ➤ *Sin & death entered the world and would be spread to all mankind (as mankind would be birthed through the loins of man).*

The sin of Adam unleashed the authority of hell on all mankind!

The apostle Paul marvelously summarized these events in only ten verses of scripture in ***Romans 5:12-21***. Powerful spiritual principles are resident within each of these three consequences of Adam's sin. We need to understand these *"...principles..."* to live healthy successful lives in Christ while we are here on earth. The three principles are:

1

THE RIDDLE

Principle One: *Sin causes separation from God.*

Principle Two: *You become a slave of the one to whom you yield.*

> *"Do you not know that to whom you present your-selves slaves to obey, you are that one's slaves whom you obey, whether of sin leading to death, or of obe-dience leading to righteousness?"* **Romans 6:16**

Principle Three: *Sin does not just affect the sinner.*

Note: The remainder of the book will be "...built..." around these three principles.

The fall of the man Adam, the need for Jesus as the last Adam, the New Covenant, Christ's provisions for healthy relationships within His church, and so many more areas to which we have been blinded were set in motion as a result of *"...sin..."*. The enemy, as the god of this world, a role established as a result of Adam's sin, has by his subtle craftiness, deceived a large segment of the church into believing inaccurately about sin. However, we will only *"...mention..."* the enemy and his deceptions, we will focus on truth from the Lord regarding sin and His provisions to deal with it effectively. Once we understand and embrace the Lord's way, our submission to Jesus as the supreme authority in our lives on the subject will cause any other way, from any other source, to be eliminated for all who are submitted to Jesus as Lord.

We simply must make Jesus supreme in authority as the practice of our lives.

Many of the sayings of the church on the earth today regarding the subject of sin demonstrate the bondage of the church in the matter.

"It's just too hard!"

"No one can overcome sin while living on the earth."

"We are just human."

"Not even the apostle Paul could overcome sin."

"Sin is not that big-a-deal."

"Do you sin?"

"Oh, I know, but..."

"I still sin, but God knows my heart."

"Well, so-in-so minister sins..."

If sin causes any degree of separation from our God, or any measure of death in our lives, or any shift of oversight to the enemy over us, we should be asking, seeking, and knocking for ways to overcome it, not for loopholes to continue in it or justify it. ***Oh, how deceived we have been!***

In order to begin to change our perspective of sin and how to deal with it, we must understand what sin is so we know if we are sinning or not.

THE RIDDLE

Strong's Exhaustive Concordance of The Bible lists term number *2398 chata* as the Hebrew word translated in the Old Testament of the Bible as *"...sin..."*, and defines the term as:

> *2398 chata* a prim. root; prob. to miss; hence (fig. and gen.) to *sin*; by infer. to *forfeit, lack, expiate, repent, (causat.) lead astray, condemn*: -- bear the blame, cleanse, commit [sin], by fault, harm he hath cone, loss, miss, (make) offend (-er), offer for sin, purge, purify (self), make reconciliation, (cause, make) sin (-ful, -ness), trespass.

Strong's lists term *266 hamartia* as the Greek word translated in the New Testament of the Bible as *"...sin..."*, and defines the term as:

> *266 hamartia* from *264*; a *sin* (prop.abstr.): -- offence, sin (-ful).

> *264 hamartano* perh. from *1* (as a neg. particle) and the base of *3313*; prop. to miss the mark (and so *not share* in the prize), i.e. (fig.) to err, esp. (mor.) to *sin*: -- for your faults, offend, sin, trespass.

The concept of *"...miss..."* in the Hebrew definition and *"...miss the mark..."* in the Greek definition help us better understand what sin is. To *"...miss..."* or *"...miss the mark..."* implies that the person aiming knew at what they were aiming. We have already learned from Paul's writings to the church at Rome *(Romans 5:12-21)* that Adam's actions regarding God's will for him were identified as *"...sin..."*. Consider the slightly different terms used by Paul when referring to Adam's sin:

*"...as through one man's **offence** (3900)..."*
("...offence..." KJV / "...offense..." NKJV)
Romans 5:18

*"...as by one man's **disobedience** (3876)..."*
Romans 5:19

3900 paraptoma from *3825;* a *side-slip* (lapse or deviation), i.e. (unintentional) error or (willful) transgression: fall, fault, offence, sin, trespass.

3876 parakoe from *3878; inattention,* i.e. (by impl.) *disobedience:* -- disobedience

Strong's Exhaustive Concordance of the Bible

Adam *"...disobeyed..."* God regarding God's will for his life. This disobedience was called *"...sin..."*. Perhaps we can simplify our task in considering sin by constructing a simple definition easy to use in relation to sin.

Sin is a violation of the known will of God.

A believer sits down at a Thanksgiving dinner with his family. Foods that are not common for ordinary meals are present. Before the end of the meal the believer's flesh, desiring the delicious foods not ordinarily available, has enticed him to eat a lot more than he should eat. He pushes away from the table feeling nauseous saying, *"I ate too much"*. This believer violated the known will of God which is not to eat so much food in excess that you become nauseated.

It is profoundly important to understand that God's will for Adam was not some arbitrary whim contrived by an uncaring God who simply desired to demonstrate His authority and

5

control over the man He had just created. Consider God's reason why He willed for Adam not to eat of the fruit of the tree of the knowledge of good and evil.

> *"And the Lord God commanded the man, saying, "Of every tree of the garden you may freely eat; but of the tree of the knowledge of good and evil you shall not eat, for in the day that you eat of it you shall surely die."*
>
> **Genesis 2:16,17**

While no little theological debate has been made over this command and the origin of the actual tree itself, there is one thing of which we can be certain: *If God did not care whether Adam lived or died, He would not have had a conversation about the tree.* **God did not desire for Adam to die!** The means for Adam to stay alive and not die was to simply do the will of God in the matter. All other debate on God's command or the origin of the tree is unnecessary for our topic.

Sin entered into the world through the first man Adam and brought with it death! Immediately after Adam's yielding to an authority other than God was complete, transfer of rule over all the works of God's hands passed from Adam to Satan, and Satan became the god of this world. Every person born on the earth through the loins of man partakes of the first man Adam's sin and is born into the world where Satan is ruler. Sin and death passes on to all men through the man Adam. Scripture is clear in these matters. Eve fell into transgression through deception. The sin by which all men are overwhelmed was Adam's because without deception he knew what he was doing and did it anyway *(I Timothy 2:14)*. Sin passing on to

6

all mankind through the "...*man*..." Adam is very significant in God's plans to redeem man. Jesus was conceived by the Holy Spirit and born of a virgin without involvement of a "...*man*..." so that sin and death did not pass into Jesus. Jesus was born without sin but had to live above sin to remain the sinless Lamb of God designed to take away the sin of the world.

An exception to this law of sin and death takes place within the home of parents who have been redeemed from the law of sin and death. Their child partakes of the redemption of the parents until the child is able to make the decision to submit to Jesus as supreme in authority in his own individual life. No one can be born again for another person, but the mercy and grace of the Lord allows the redemption of a father and or mother to cover their child until the child can make their own decision *(See I Corinthians 7:10-16)*.

THE RIDDLE

Chapter Two

THE CONSEQUENCES OF SIN

Although we have seen the catastrophic consequences of Adam's sin, causing sin and death to pass on to all mankind, we need to see the consequences of sin in our individual lives. Paul wrote *"...the wages of sin is death..." (**Romans 5:23**)*, but how does that apply to us practically, or does it even apply to us today? Consider the context from which these few words from scripture are taken to begin to answer these questions.

In Paul's writings to the church at Rome he wrote,

> *"...do not let sin reign in your mortal body, that you should obey it in its lusts. And do not present your members as instruments of unrighteousness to sin, but present yourselves to God as being alive from the dead, and your members as instruments of righteousness to God. For sin shall not have dominion over you, for you are not under law but under grace. What then? Shall we sin because we are not under law but under grace? Certainly not! Do you not know that to whom you present yourselves slaves to obey, you are that one's slaves whom you obey, whether of sin leading to death, or of obedience leading to righteousness? But God be thanked that though you were slaves of sin..." **Romans 6:12-17***

Sin has the ability to enslave us
so that it reigns in our mortal bodies.

Tobacco products provide us with a wonderful illustration here. The Surgeon General of the United States requires all tobacco products to include a health warning. We know the addictive quality and health hazard of tobacco to the user. Typically, when a person has used tobacco products for any length of time and desires to quit using, he faces an extremely difficult time quitting. Stop-smoking products have become a huge business. If the tobacco user is a Christian, he may even seek help such as prayer and or deliverance to break the nicotine habit. Repentance for using tobacco products is seldom a consideration.

However, because Jesus died to deliver us from the law of sin and death, any product we use that could produce death in us would violate the known will of God. If this is the case, then, tobacco use is a sin. Because it is sin the user would become enslaved to it; it would become his master. A simple acknowledgement that his tobacco use is sin, followed by repentance done in faith, and acceptance of forgiveness from the Lord would deliver the captive from his enslavement to sin and captivity of the devil. This believer would still have to learn how to walk in the spirit so as not to yield to the lusts of his flesh, but Jesus would have taken his sin away, not just covered it.

We see a similar understanding of "...sin..." to Paul's letter to Rome in God's conversation with Cain in the Old Testament. The content of this conversation deals with Cain and Abel giving offerings to God. God respected Abel and his offering but not Cain and his offering.

THE RIDDLE

"...And the Lord respected Abel and his offering, but He did not respect Cain and his offering. And Cain was very angry, and his countenance fell. So the Lord said to Cain, "Why are you angry? And why has your countenance fallen? If you do well, will you not be accepted? And if you do not do well, sin lies at the door. And its desire is for you, but you should rule over it."

Genesis 4:4-7

The understanding we gain here is of profound importance! In both references, **Romans 6:12-17** and **Genesis 4:4-7**, God the Holy Spirit inspired the writers, Paul and Moses, to present sin as if it were a sentient being having desires to rule over man.

In Paul's letter to the church at Rome this concept is emphasized in an extraordinary manner. Paul is presenting sin from the perspective that the issue is not for man not to commit an act of sin, but rather not to present himself as a slave to obey sin. The difference between sin as a singular act that man commits versus sin as an entity to whom man can submit is huge.

James adds another piece to our understanding in his letter to the believers who are part of the twelve tribes scattered abroad:

"Blessed is the man who endures temptation; for when he has been approved, he will receive the crown of life which the Lord has promised to those who love Him. Let no one say when he is tempted, "I am tempted by God"; for God cannot be tempted by evil, nor does He Himself tempt anyone. But each one is tempted when he

is drawn away by his own desires and enticed. Then, when desire has conceived, it gives birth to sin; and sin, when it is full-grown, brings forth death..."
James 1:12-15

The bait of sin is the desire of man's flesh. The desires of the flesh are not sin themselves, but they can lead to sin. Jesus Himself demonstrated desires of the flesh during His temptation in the wilderness. At the end of His forty day fast ordained by God where food had been forbidden, scripture says Jesus *"...hungered...".* Hunger at the end of a forty day fast clearly identifies desires of the flesh. These desires in Jesus' flesh were not sin, or Jesus could not have been the sinless Lamb of God to take away the sin of the world. Sin desired to rule over Jesus, but Jesus did not present Himself as a slave to obey sin.

The understanding available here is that *"...desires of the flesh..."* do not equal sin by themselves. Sin is an external entity that will produce death if man submits himself to obey. Certainly, if a man submits himself as a slave to obey sin, that sin becomes an internal part of the man, ruling over him. Jesus said,

"...whoever looks at a woman to lust for her has already committed adultery with her in his heart..."
Matthew 5:28

A man who has committed adultery with a woman in his heart may never actually commit the physical act of adultery, but he is nevertheless considered an adulterer by the Lord because of the sin of adultery dwelling inside of him.

According to the inspiration from God under which James wrote, desires of the flesh themselves are not sin unless conception takes place. Conception requires two of man's parts to come together. If a man begins to think on the desires of his flesh in a wanton fashion, then conception takes place within the man and sin results. Sin would then dwell within the man. Under the old covenant it was impossible for man to be free from the law of sin and death because he only had his own power to use in an effort to rule over the weakness of his flesh. No matter how hard man tried to overcome sin he could not. He was bound by the law of sin and death. According to scripture this is precisely why a new covenant was needed, a covenant no longer based on the power of man, but rather the power of God working in man.

Paul contrasted man's life under the old covenant with man's life under the new covenant. From the beginning of his letter to the church at Rome Paul discussed faith and life in the new covenant. He emphasized the glory that exists in being made free from the law of sin and death. Then in chapter seven he *transitions back* to life under the old covenant using his own life as illustration to help us see the difference between the old and the new covenants. In chapter seven, beginning with verse seven, he explains how the Law of God worked in the old covenant to make sin appear as sin. Under the old covenant once Paul had seen what sin was and endeavored to overcome it, he saw the hopelessness of his own power to make him free from the law of sin and death while living under the old covenant. He presents such a picture of despair trying to live life under the old covenant using his own life as illustration; it is horrific.

CONSEQUENCES OF SIN

"Do you not know, brethren (for I speak to those who know the law), that the law has dominion over a man as long as he lives? For the woman who has a husband is bound by the law to her husband as long as he lives. But if the husband dies, she is released from the law of her husband. So then, if, while her husband lives, she marries another man, she will be called an adulteress; but if her husband dies, she is free from that law, so that she is no adulteress, though she has married another man. Therefore, my brethren, you also have become dead to the law through the body of Christ, that you may be married to another, to Him who was raised from the dead, that we should bear fruit to God. For when we were in the flesh, the sinful passions which were aroused by the law were at work in our members to bear fruit to death. But now we have been delivered from the law, having died to what we were held by, so that we should serve in the newness of the Spirit and not in the letter. What shall we say then? Is the law sin? Certainly not! On the contrary, I would not have known sin except through the law. For I would not have known covetousness unless the law said, "You shall not covet." But sin, taking opportunity by the commandment, produced in me all manner of evil desire. For apart from the law sin was dead. I was alive once without the law, but when the commandment came, sin revived and I died. And the commandment, which was to bring life, I found to bring death. For sin, taking occasion by the commandment, deceived me, and by it killed me. Therefore the law is holy, and the commandment holy and just and good. Has then what is good become death to me? Certainly not! But sin, that it might appear sin, was producing death in me through what is good, so that sin through the commandment might become exceeding sinful. For we know that the law is spiritual, but I am carnal, sold under sin. For what I am doing, I do not understand. For what I will to do, that I do not practice; but what I hate, that I do. If, then, I do what I will not to do, I agree with the law that it is good. But now, it is no longer I who do it, but sin

that dwells in me. For I know that in me (that is, in my flesh) nothing good dwells; for to will is present with me, but how to perform what is good I do not find. For the good that I will to do, I do not do; but the evil I will not to do, that I practice. Now if I do what I will not to do, it is no longer I who do it, but sin that dwells in me. I find then a law, that evil is present with me, the one who wills to do good. For I delight in the law of God according to the inward man. But I see another law in my members, warring against the law of my mind, and bringing me into captivity to the law of sin which is in my members. O wretched man that I am! Who will deliver me from this body of death? I thank God through Jesus Christ our Lord! So then, with the mind I myself serve the law of God, but with the flesh the law of sin. There is therefore now no condemnation to those who are in Christ Jesus, who do not walk according to the flesh, but according to the Spirit. For the law of the Spirit of life in Christ Jesus has made me free from the law of sin and death. ..." **Romans 7:1-8:2**

Life under the old covenant was lived in the power of man. Man, in his own power, simply could not overcome the law of sin and death; it was hopeless. As mere men no matter how hard we try to overcome sin in our lives, we cannot. As mere men living in our own power, we will remain slaves to sin as long as we live in our unglorified natural bodies. Sin will have dominion over us.

But thank God, God made a new covenant available to us established on better promises than the old covenant. The better promises are based on man having access to the power of God as the means to live free from the law of sin and death. A new covenant man who is truly born again is freed from sin.

The new covenant man is dead to sin and the control of sin and free to live free from sin as a way of life in Christ Jesus. This freedom is a gift from our God. However, every believer who has become a recipient of this free gift must learn to walk out his salvation in fear and trembling on a daily basis. It is possible for a believer who has been freed from sin to return to sin, such as the repentant tobacco user receiving forgiveness, healing, and deliverance from tobacco products starting to use again.

Whenever a believer submits himself to sin, a dreadful thing occurs; that believer becomes a *"...slave..."* to sin. When Paul wrote about this revelation to the church at Rome, he wrote in such a manner to imply he was writing revelation the church should already know.

> *"Do you not know that to whom you present yourselves slaves (1401) to obey, you are that one's slaves (1401) whom you obey, whether of sin leading to death, or of obedience leading to righteousness?"* **Romans 6:16**

> *1401 doulos* from *1210*; a *slave* (lit. or fig., invol. or vol.: frequently therefore in a qualified sense of *subjection* or *subserviency*): -- bond (-man), servant.

Strong's Exhaustive Concordance of the Bible

If a born-again believer turns back to sin, he does so as a direct result of *"...being drawn away by his own desires and enticed..." (See James 1:12-15)*. One thing we must absolutely establish, sin does not sneak up on you, bonk you on the head, and drag you off into captivity like a cave-man capturing a wife. This seems to be the subtle corruption the enemy has perpetuated amongst believers today, that sin is so powerful it can overtake you and make you yield.

THE RIDDLE

The law of the spirit of life in Christ Jesus that has made us free from the law of sin and death is infinitely more powerful than the law of sin and death from which we have been made free. The reason the church has not lived free of sin on the earth is not because sin is so powerful or because our flesh is so weak, but rather, *at least in part*, because the church has been so deceived by the subtle devices of the enemy. We must unravel the riddle of sin, forgiveness, repentance, and restoration of relationship so we may see these things from God's perspective. We have been *"...made free..."* from the law of sin and death so we may *"...live free..."* from the law of sin and death!

Paul adds a new ingredient to our understanding in his letter to Timothy. In giving Timothy instructions regarding approved and disapproved workers in ministry Paul wrote...

> *"...A servant of the Lord must not quarrel but be gentle to all, able to teach, patient, in humility correcting those who are in opposition (KJV translates "...who are in opposition..." as "...those that oppose themselves...").*
> *If God perhaps will grant them repentance, so that they may know the truth, and that they may come to their senses and escape the snare (3803) of the devil, having been taken captive (2221) by him to do his will..."*
> **II Timothy 2:24-26**

3803 pagis from *4078*; a *trap* (as *fastened* by a noose or notch); fig. a *trick* or *stratagem* (*temptation*): -- snare.

2221 zogreo from the same as *2226* and *64*; to *take alive* (*make a prisoner of war*), i.e.. (fig.) to *capture* or *ensnare*: -- take captive, catch.

Strong's Exhaustive Concordance of the Bible

CONSEQUENCES OF SIN

If a believer yields to sin again in his life anytime after new birth, it is imperative that we understand such a believer becomes a *"...prisoner of war..."* with the devil as his captor. This is not good! Is there any way your imagination allows you to view Abba, your Father, leaving you, His son, to the mercies of the devil? Or can you conjure up any type of thought to consider how God could send His only begotten Son to die for us as the only way to redeem us from the law of sin and death, and then, leave us to live out our daily lives in our own power here on earth where Satan is still god of this world? We must awaken to these lies!

God has made a way for us to live free from the law of sin and death from which He delivered us at the time of our new birth. Jesus was the means to deliver us through new birth, and Jesus is the means for us to overcome sin after we have been born again. We must believe this simple truth and find His way to live free from the law of sin and death from which He delivered us! *Now, what is His way?*

Consider Paul's instruction to Timothy as the first step toward gaining adequate understanding in finding the way of the Lord. Paul wrote,

> *"...A servant of the Lord must not quarrel but be gentle to all, able to teach, patient, in humility correcting those who are in opposition (KJV translates "...who are in opposition..." as "...those that oppose themselves..."). If God perhaps will grant them repentance, so that they may know the truth, and that they may come to their senses and escape the snare (3803) of the devil, having been taken captive (2221) by him to do his will..."*
> **II Timothy 2:24-26**

Firstly, we see that a person who yields to sin opposes himself as the KJV translation states. This opposition to self is easy to see as scripture teaches the sinning brother is personally and individually taken captive by the enemy. The enemy has corrupted the concept of sin by making it seem the greatest harm done by the person sinning is to others. Absolutely not! The persons sinned against do not go into a satanic trap nor do they become enslaved by sin. The person who sins is the one who has Satan as his captor and becomes enslaved by sin.

Our first step must be to change our mind-set about whose need takes priority in a relationship where sin is involved, the one who sinned or the one sinned against. Surely both have needs, but the one who sinned needs a way to be freed from Satan as his captor and released from his enslavement to sin. The one who is sinned against needs a way to overcome emotional or physical conditions caused as a result of the sin against him. Again, both needs are legitimate, but a person enslaved by the law of sin and death with the devil as his captor must take priority with a motive to help him be freed from his bondage.

The means to help the captive brother is to show him the truth he has violated. We created a simple definition of *"...sin as a violation of the known will of God...".* The sin a brother *(This must be a believer walking together with you as a part of the church.)* has committed may be against you personally or simply a violation of the will of God in some other area of life. Perhaps the easiest of the two of these to see is if your brother sins against you personally. Jesus gave an instruction to the church about the means to deal with sin if a brother has committed sin against you personally. Matthew recorded Jesus as saying,

"Moreover if your brother sins against you, go and tell him his fault between you and him alone. If he hears you, you have gained your brother. But if he will not hear, take with you one or two more, that by the mouth of two or three witnesses every word may be established. And if he refuses to hear them, tell it to the church. But if he refuses even to hear the church, let him be to you like a heathen and a tax collector. Assuredly, I say to you, whatever you bind on earth will be bound in heaven, and whatever you loose on earth will be loosed in heaven. Again I say to you that if two of you agree on earth concerning anything that they ask, it will be done for them by My Father in heaven. For where two or three are gathered together in My name, I am there in the midst of them." **Matthew 18:15-20**

The first step in helping a sinning brother is to *"...go and tell him his fault between you and him alone..."*. **This step is not an option; it is a commandment from the Lord!** The reason for telling the sinning brother exactly what he has done that violated the will of God is to make sure he knows what he has done and to make sure that what he has done actually violated the known will of God. Too often a brother simply aggravates our soul because his personality is not likable to us, but his actions do not actually violate the known will of God.

My wife and I were Bible translation personnel living in a distant foreign land with Wycliffe Bible Translators. Life on the foreign field occasionally required group living conditions. I remember one such situation where we were partaking of meals all together in one common building for several weeks.

I was about to invoke *Matthew 18:15-20* toward one of the persons with whom we were required to be grouped. I told the Lord my intent and to my pleasant surprise He said, *"Good, that is My will."* I was feeling so affirmed and so spiritual. Then, He began to speak to me about the matter. He said, *"Before you go make sure you know what the person's sin is."* I was sure that would not be a problem. So, He asked me, *"What exactly is their sin?"* I thought and stammered momentarily, only to realize their actions had not violated the will of God; they were merely an aggravation to my soul. The real need for change was in me. I needed to mature to a place where the person's actions did not *"...aggravate..."* me. I needed to learn to accept the diversity of personalities that exist within the body of Christ and to see the richness in them. Or at the very least to see the Lord was not requiring me to become best friends with this person, just to allow them to be who they were, as long as that did not violate the known will of God.

Jesus' commandment to *"...go and tell him his fault between you and him alone..."* will require us to consider our brother's actions to make absolutely sure he has actually violated the known will of God. In every way Jesus' way will help to improve our relationships with one another if we keep our hearts submitted to the Lord and understand how much His will is designed to help us.

Once we have told our brother the truth regarding his violation of the known will of God, hopefully he will *"...come to his senses..."* and see what he has done to himself, having yielded to sin and has become enslaved by it, and has entered into a satanic trap from which he sees his need to be freed. Under these conditions we help walk out our brother's repentance, extend forgiveness, and we have gained our brother freed from his satanic trap.

If our brother refuses to hear us and rejects our motive to help him, then Jesus tells us to take two or three more with us to repeat the process. Taking two or three more with us does not change our motive. Our motive still remains desire to help our brother be freed from the satanic trap. Taking two or three more with us is as much for our sake as for the sake of the sinning brother. The two or three who go with us can help make sure our motive is pure before we go and remains pure while we are with our sinning brother. If our brother refuses to hear all of us together, then we repeat the process before the entire church. If our sinning brother refuses to hear even the entire church, Jesus requires the basis of our relationship to change. We must relate to him *"...like a heathen and a tax collector..."*.

Jesus as supreme in authority over the church, having preeminence in all things to the church, is the one requiring these actions. Everything Jesus does as **Preeminent Lord** over the church is to promote life within the church. Absolutely nothing Jesus wills is punitive toward any member of His body. Jesus wills for the brother who has become enslaved by sin and taken captive by the devil to be set free! However, if the brother refuses to submit to the supreme authority of Jesus as the Head of His own body, and to the members of His body who have followed Jesus' instructions regarding how to deal with the sinning brother, then the sinning brother's unrepentant actions must not be allowed to rule in the House of the Lord.

This must become indelibly clear in our hearts and minds, *"...a brother who has become enslaved by sin and taken captive by the devil needs our help!"* Unless we go to such a brother exactly as Jesus has ordained disaster will follow. Scripture is simple, clear, and easily understandable in this matter:

> *"Brethren, if a man is overtaken in any trespass, you who are **spiritual** restore such a one in a spirit of gentleness, considering yourself lest you also be tempted. Bear one another's burdens, and so fulfill the law of Christ. For if anyone thinks himself to be something when he is nothing, he deceives himself..."* **Galatians 6:1-3**

According to the way of the Lord, going to a sinning brother must be motivated by our desire to help the sinning brother extricate himself from his satanic trap and his enslavement of sin. The person going to such a sinning brother must be *"...spiritual..."* himself before he can determine to go to the sinning brother. Determining whether or not you are spiritual before you go to your brother must not be a subjective or a difficult thing to do. It should be easy to make such a determination by answering just *one* question:

Is my motive to help my brother?

If the answer to this question is *"...no..."* or if you are not sure, then you must not approach your sinning brother. *You* will make matters worse and *"...disaster will follow..."!*

Your sinning brother needs your "...help...", he does not need to help you while he suffers enslavement to sin and captivity of the devil!

Note: Instructions for us to deal with a sinning brother, or help restore a brother overtaken in any trespass, must be limited to the scope of dealing with a brother who desires to walk together with us as a part of the church. These instructions are absolutely "...not..." to be applied to a person who has chosen to run away from Christ, us individually, and the church corporately. Jesus' instructions are not for us to "...straighten out..." a person who has chosen to run away. They are to help a brother who has sinned but who still remains in our midst.

Chapter Three

SPIRITUAL REQUIREMENT

We must take one more look at the requirements for the person going to help a sinning brother. Paul's instructions to the church at Galatia for the person who is *"...spiritual..."* to help restore one who is overtaken with any trespass is not maturity based. We cannot equate a person's condition as *"...spiritual..."* to that of growth spiritually. This has been another of the subtle devices the enemy has used to corrupt the will of the Lord.

A person who is *"...spiritual..."* is simply any believer who has chosen spiritual as a way of life. The new covenant is designed to work for spiritual people. The alternative to spiritual people is carnal people. Paul wrote some amazing things regarding the difference between spiritual and carnal to the church at Rome.

"There is therefore now no condemnation to those who are in Christ Jesus, who do not walk according to the flesh, but according to the spirit. For the law of the spirit of life in Christ Jesus has made me free from the law of sin and death. For what the law could not do in that it was weak through the flesh, God did by sending His own Son in the likeness of sinful flesh, on account of sin: He condemned sin in the flesh, that the righteous requirement of the law might be fulfilled in us who do not walk according to the flesh but according to the spirit. For those who live according to the flesh set their minds on the things of the flesh, but those who live according

to the spirit, the things of the spirit. For to be carnally minded is death, but to be spiritually minded is life and peace. Because the carnal mind is enmity against God; for it is not subject to the law of God nor indeed can be..." **Romans 8:1-7**

Because this concept has been corrupted and must be re-established back into the church, more scriptural illustrations are required here to help distinguish the difference between life lived as a mere man versus life lived as a spiritual man.

"O foolish Galatians! Who has bewitched you that you should not obey the truth, before whose eyes Jesus Christ was clearly portrayed among you as crucified? This only I want to learn from you. Did you receive the Spirit by the works of the law, or by the hearing of faith? Are you so foolish? Having begun in the spirit, are you now being made perfect by the flesh?" **Galatians 3:1-3**

"And I, brethren, could not speak to you as to spiritual people but as to carnal, as to babes in Christ. I fed you with milk and not with solid food; for until now you were not able to receive it, and even now you are still not able; for you are still carnal. For where there are envy, strife, and divisions among you, are you not carnal and behaving like mere men?" **I Corinthians 3:1-3**

The new covenant simply will not work for a person who lives as a mere man. Every facet of the new covenant requires new creatures in Christ to walk as spiritual men, rather than as mere men. What Paul told the church at Galatia, *"...if a man is overtaken in any trespass, you who are spiritual restore such a one..."* applies to all believers who are spiritually minded.

Consider Jesus' instructions again regarding dealing with a sinning brother as recorded by Matthew. Jesus said, *"...if your brother sins against you, go and tell him his fault between you and him alone..."*. Jesus did not say only those who are spiritually mature go to your brother who has sinned against you and tell him his fault. Going to your brother who has sinned against you is a *"...fundamental..."* component of the new covenant and must apply to all believers who have practical relationships with one another.

The purpose for going to your sinning brother who has sinned against you is not to *"...straighten him out..."*, or to *"...disciple him..."*, but rather to deal with a specific sin he has committed which has caused him to be enslaved to sin and captured by the devil. The motive for going to him is love for him and a desire to see him free! The motive is to help your brother. The need to be *"...spiritual..."* as the foundation upon which you go to your sinning brother is to make sure you are going as a new covenant flesh and bone part of Christ's body operating in faith.

The instant a believer who has been sinned against stops being *"...spiritual..."* in his involvement with his sinning brother, the believer-who-has-been-sinned-against's motive will change to less than the will of God. The change will be from spiritual to mere man minded which opens the door to the enemy, and the enemy will most certainly rule in the relationship. Consider Paul's letter to the mere man-minded church at Corinth:

THE RIDDLE

> *"And I, brethren, could not speak to you as to spiritual people but as to carnal, as to babes in Christ. I fed you with milk and not with solid food; for until now you were not able to receive it, and even now you are still not able; for you are still carnal. For where there are envy, strife, and divisions among you, are you not carnal and behaving like mere men?..."* **I Corinthians 3:1-3**

Here, God the Holy Spirit inspired Paul to equate non-spiritual people with carnal people. The conditions which existed among these carnal people were envy, strife, and divisions. All of these conditions were direct results of the people being non-spiritual people. None of the three of these conditions are acceptable within the church, the body of Christ. The enemy has persuaded a segment of the church that it is acceptable to *"...not..."* be a spiritual person, that if you are a *"...good..."* person, and can call yourself a Christian, then you are good to go.

This mind-set has become an acceptable tradition in much of the church today: As long as you *"...go to church..."* regularly and do your best to live as a *"...good..."* person, you are okay. Nothing could be further from the truth. Look at Paul's letter to the church at Rome:

> *"...those who live according to the flesh set their minds on the things of the flesh, but those who live according to the spirit, the things of the spirit. For to be carnally minded is death, but to be spiritually minded is life and peace. Because the carnal mind is enmity (2189) against God; for it is not subject to the law of God, nor indeed can be. So then those who are in the flesh cannot please God..."* **Romans 8:5-8**

SPIRITUAL REQUIREMENT

2189 echtra fem. of 2190; *hostility*; by impl. a reason for *opposition*: -- enmity, hatred.

Strong's Exhaustive Concordance of the Bible

enmity - deep seated ill will such as might be felt for an enemy.

**The American Heritage Dictionary
of the English Language**

When the truth regarding a topic the enemy has corrupted is presented in an accurate loving fashion, the lies of the enemy are easily exposed. According to the revelation Paul presented to the church at Corinth by inspiration of God the Holy Spirit, a born again person who is not *"...spiritual..."* is living as a mere man and is carnal *(See **I Corinthians 3:1-3**)*. Revelation presented by Paul to the church at Rome by inspiration of the same Holy Spirit reveals that to be carnally minded is death, and perhaps worse than that the carnal mind is enmity against God.

God the Father *"...so loved the world that He gave His only begotten Son, that whoever believes in Him should not perish, but have everlasting life..." **(John 3:16)**.* This everlasting life the Father desires for us to have is not just living forever when we get to heaven. It is living the kind of life that God has while we are living here on earth.

"...this is life eternal, that they may know You, the only true God, and Jesus Christ whom You have sent..."
John 17:3

29

Everlasting life *(which is eternal life)* is based on our knowledge of God. Can you conceive of any way for our God to sacrifice His only begotten Son as the only way for us to live and not die, then make it acceptable for us to live carnally minded in death as His enemy while we live here on earth?!? This is precisely the device the enemy has in place in many many born again persons' lives. This lie must be uncovered, plucked up, cast down and removed from the people of God. We must become the spiritual people Jesus died for us to become!

I do not believe any born again person would knowingly choose to live carnally minded in death as enmity against God! Such is the nature of *"...deception..."*. A person who is deceived does not know they are deceived. They believe what they believe is the truth. Abba has made provision for us to have an **objective** standard whereby we can measure all revelation to see whether it is from God or whether it is a subtle corruption from the enemy. He has given us the written standard of the Bible. He has given us the Holy Spirit who is responsible to guide us into all truth. He has given us mature believers to rightly divide the word of truth who use the written standard, the ministry of the Holy Spirit, and confirmation of the brethren to help us objectively know truth. We can know the truth but only if our heart is turned toward the Lord and have chosen to be a spiritual person.

There is a corresponding consequence to mere-man-mindedness that does not originate from within the believer. The moment a believer begins to deal with another believer regarding the issue of sin in a mere-man manner, a signal is released into the spirit realm. This signal, like blood in the water to sharks who are always looking for prey to devour, is heard by the enemy who is always listening for just such a signal. Peter wrote about this very issue:

> *"Be sober, be vigilant; because your adversary the devil walks about like a roaring lion, seeking whom he may devour."* **I Peter 5:8**

A believer who walks like a mere man typically does not consciously walk like a mere man. In most cases a believer who is walking like a mere man is simply deceived, thinking he is spiritual. *How can a mere-man-minded believer think he is spiritual?* Simple, because he uses his own thought as the standard for his life, rather than the Christ as the living standard. Even if a believer would use the word presented in the Bible as the written standard by which he judged his own thoughts, actions, and life, it would be almost impossible for such a believer to not see the will of God regarding how to deal with a sinning brother.

Look at Jesus' instructions recorded by Matthew in this matter:

> *"...if your brother sins against you, go and tell him his fault between you and him alone..."* **Matthew 18:15**

It is absolutely impossible to misinterpret Jesus' instructions here. They are full of simplicity. Then how does any believer not see, understand, and follow these instructions? Because the mere-man-minded believer opened the door to the enemy by being mere-man-minded, and the enemy has entered this brother's thought processes and fed such a believer information that has exalted itself against the knowledge of God. This information looks like this; *"I cannot go to my brother because..."*

"Who am I to tell him anything?"

"I am not going to him; it is too hard to talk to him."

"I tried talking to him before, but he would not listen."

"I tried talking to him before, but he bit my head off."

"Well, he doesn't follow Jesus' instructions, so how can he ask me to?"

We have already determined that Jesus as supreme in authority over the church is not instructing the church to go to our brother who has sinned to punish him, nor to straighten him out, nor to disciple him. Jesus is sending us to our sinning brother because Jesus loves him and wants us to love him enough to help him be set free from his enslavement to sin and from his captivity of the devil. Jesus knows not every believer who has sinned against his brother will hear or receive the brother whom he has sinned against, nor will all repent. Jesus has made provision for this, too. He tells us exactly what to do if our brother to whom we have gone refuses to hear and repent.

"Moreover if your brother sins against you, go and tell him his fault between you and him alone. If he hears you, you have gained your brother...

...But if he will not hear you, take with you one or two more, that by the mouth of two or three witnesses every word may be established. And if he refuses to hear them, tell it to the church. But if he refuses even to hear the church, let him be to you like a heathen and a tax collector..." **Matthew 18:15-17**

Jesus' instructions here are easily understandable. Every believer could do them.

One understanding we have achieved which must be constantly remembered and held in high esteem in our knowledge of God:

> *Jesus is not interested in punishing a sinning believer. He is interested in helping him free himself of his enslavement to sin and his captivity of the devil.*

This is pivotal in our approach to dealing with a sinning brother. We love our brother. Our motive in going to him is to *"...help him..."!* Even if the sin our brother committed against us hurt us, our priority is to help free our brother from his enslavement to sin and his captivity of the devil. Jesus has provision for us to receive ministry to deal with our hurts, too, but our priority is to help our brother be freed from his captivity involving the devil.

Whether two or three more are involved in going with us to our brother who has sinned against us, or even involving the whole church, we are confident all of Jesus' instructions have the sinning brother's freedom as His priority. The sinning brother could reject the input from the brother he has sinned against when the sinned-against brother comes to him alone to tell him his fault. The sinning brother could think the sinned-against brother is just retaliating for challenges in their relationship. But, the moment two or three more become involved, and then the whole church, the sinning brother would have the broadest possible base of *"...objective..."* input for him to be able to see that his actions against his brother were actually sin. We are most interested in our brother coming to the knowledge of the truth, repenting, and extricating himself from the snare of the devil so we may gain our brother!

Only a spiritual person will be able to see and understand Jesus' motive for us to follow the instructions exactly as He has given them. A mere-man-minded person will find every reason and excuse why Jesus' instructions either do not apply to him or how he has already followed Jesus' instructions when, in reality, he has not. A mere-man-minded person is a dangerous person in the church because his own thoughts are the standard by which he judges his own actions and life and because he is easy prey for the enemy to *"...use..."* against the people of God. The new covenant simply will not work for a person who lives as a mere man. Every facet of the new covenant requires new creatures in Christ to walk as spiritual men, rather than as mere men.

Chapter Four

FORGIVENESS WITHOUT REPENTANCE IS DEAD TO RESTORE RELATIONSHIP

Faith is a gift from God, and yet James wrote by inspiration from the same God who gave faith as a gift that *"...faith without works is dead..."* *(James 2:26 See context, verses 14-26)*. James did not write that faith is dead. He wrote that faith *"...without works..."* is dead. The clear meaning throughout the entire context of James chapter two, verse fourteen through verse twenty-six, is that faith was not given by God as an end. It was given by God as the means to accomplish certain ends.

God endowed faith with divine abilities so that the recipients of faith could employ faith to live successfully in-Christ and to accomplish whatever God willed for them to *"...do..."*. Because faith as a gift from God originates in the spirit world and not in this natural world, those who have been given this marvelous gift must walk as spiritual people to be able to learn how to use faith in the spirit. Everyone has natural faith, but not everyone has faith as a gift from God *(See II Thessalonians 3:1,2)*. Although both natural world faith and spirit world faith work similarly, natural world faith will not accomplish God's will. That is why God gave spirit world faith to us!

THE RIDDLE

Forgiveness is like faith in at least two ways: forgiveness can be both natural world and spirit world based; and forgiveness is dead without repentance to accomplish restoration of relationship. Forgiveness is defined as:

1. to give up resentment against or the desire to punish; to stop being angry with; to pardon.
2. to give up all claim to punish or exact penalty for (an offense); to overlook.
3. to cancel or remit, as a debt, fine, or penalty.

Syn. - pardon, absolve, remit, cancel, release.

Webster's New Universal Unabridged Dictionary

All men in the natural world, saved or not, have the ability to forgive. However, the forgiveness a saved person has, and is capable of giving, is God's provision to us founded on the redeeming blood of the Christ. God's provision of forgiveness takes sin away through Christ; natural world forgiveness does not. Only one who is redeemed walking as a spiritual person can employ the forgiveness given by God empowered with divine abilities.

It is essential that we have forgiveness readily available and easily given to anyone who sins against us. Jesus taught His disciples how to pray, giving them what we know as The Lord's Prayer *(Matthew 6:7-13)*. Immediately following this model prayer Jesus continued with a very important understanding regarding forgiveness *(verses 14 & 15)*. Matthew records Jesus as saying in these two verses:

FORGIVENESS

"For if you forgive men their trespasses, your heavenly Father will also forgive you. But if you do not forgive men their trespasses, neither will your Father forgive your trespasses." **Matthew 6:14,15**

Jesus presents a frightening understanding in these two verses. Our God is not willing to *"...forgive..."* us of our sins if we are not willing to *"...forgive..."* others who have sinned against us. Without the understanding contained in this revelation it is impossible to live a healthy life in Christ. We have already been made to understand that the person who sins is enslaved by sin, captured by the devil, and has some measure of death at work within his life as a result of his sin. The only redemption from enslavement, captivity, and death is forgiveness from God. However, Jesus Himself told us very plainly that if we do not forgive others who have sinned against us, God will not forgive us our sins. Put in other words...

If we do not forgive others who have sinned against us, we cannot be redeemed from our enslavement, captivity, and death!

The person who is unwilling to forgive others keeps himself from being forgiven. Who would do such an unthinkable thing? *...only a person who does not know the truth in the matter!*

The first *"...function..."* of forgiveness as a gift from God is to keep our heart free from unforgiveness and open to receive forgiveness from God. Application of forgiveness in this way has to do with keeping our personal relationship with our God healthy. This first function of forgiveness does not directly involve the one who has sinned against us. It is simply an application of forgiveness done within our own heart.

As we have already seen the effects of sin on an individual are very destructive. The one who sins becomes enslaved by sin and taken captive by the devil.

> *"Do you not know that to whom you present yourselves slaves to obey, you are that one's slaves whom you obey, whether of sin leading to death, or of obedience leading to righteousness?"* **Romans 6:16**

> *"...In humility correcting those who are in opposition (...oppose themselves... KJV Version), if God perhaps will grant them repentance, so that they may know the truth, and that they may come to their senses and escape the snare of the devil, having been taken captive by him to do his will..."* **II Timothy 2:25,26**

In addition to these destructive consequences in the sinning brother's life, his relationship with the church changes. Contained within Jesus' instructions on how to deal with a sinning brother is a powerful clue to the type of change which occurs in our relationship as a result of our brother's sin.

> *"Moreover if your brother sins against you, go and tell him his fault between you and him alone. If he hears you, you have gained (2770) your brother..."*

> **2770 kerdaino** from *2771*; to *gain* (lit. or fig.): -- (get) gain, win.

The Greek term *"...kerdaino..."* for which the English word *"...gained..."* is translated is defined in **Strong's Exhaustive Concordance of the Bible** as *"...(get) gain, win..."*. In both terms, gain and win, there is an implied meaning that the thing you desire to gain or win you do not currently have; you must gain it or win it. In order to *"...gain your brother..."* there must be some degree of separation between him and the church requiring us to gain or win him back.

One of the immediate consequences of Adam's sin was separation from His creator. When a believer sins and is enslaved by sin, taken captive by the devil, and partakes of a measure of death, there is some degree of separation between him and the church. If a natural person violates the law, is arrested, and convicted, he will be separated from his family as a result of his violation of the law. He is still loved by his family and still a part of his family, but he is definitely going to be separated from them. This is very similar to what happens to the believer who sins: He is still born again; he is still loved by the church, but he is taken captive by the devil and needs to be set free in order to be restored back to the church.

The enemy has corrupted the revelation of sin in such a manner so as to convince people sin is inevitable, and God understands. The general *"...corrupt..."* consensus is, *"Everyone sins; it is just impossible not to sin, but God knows our heart."* Presenting an accurate revelation of sin, its destructive quality, and our need to overcome it has caused people to resist beyond reason. The voice of their resistance sounds like, *"So, if sin is that bad and a person sins, it means..."*

"...they are no longer born again?"

"...they are going to hell?"

"...God does not love them anymore?"

"...that no one is saved, because everyone sins?"

Absolutely none of these things are true. We have already seen Jesus is not interested in punishing a sinning believer. He is interested in helping him be freed of his enslavement to sin and his captivity of the devil. Jesus and all who are willing to follow Jesus' instructions are motivated by love for the sinning brother and a desire to see him freed because sin produces such devastating effects in the one who sins.

The second *"...function..."* of forgiveness actually involves the sinning brother. Jesus' motives for sending us to *"...tell him his fault..."* and our motives for going are love for our brother, desire to see him freed, and that we may gain our brother. Before we go to our sinning brother there is a crucial component of the process in dealing with him we must understand.

Immediately following Jesus instructions on dealing with a sinning brother scripture says...

> *"Then Peter came to Him and said, "Lord, how often shall my brother sin against me, and I forgive him? Up to seven times?" Jesus said to him, "I do not say to you, up to seven times, but up to seventy times seven..."*
> ***Matthew 18:21,22***

In order to make forgiveness work practically seventy times seven we must understand what the crucial component is we have already mentioned as a precursor needed before we go to our sinning brother. Luke records Jesus speaking to His disciples about the subject of sin. It is in this setting recorded by Luke that Jesus reveals the crucial component with great plainness of speech. The crucial component is *"...repentance..."*.

> *"Take heed to yourselves. If your brother sins against you, rebuke him; and **if he repents, forgive him**. And if he sins against you seven times in a day, and seven times in a day returns to you, saying, '**I repent,' you shall forgive him.**" Luke 17:3,4*

Jesus' words *"...if he repents, forgive him..."* do not nullify the first function of forgiveness. Before we even consider going to our brother who has sinned against us, we must make absolutely certain we are going as a spiritual person, that we have applied forgiveness within our own heart toward our brother, and that we understand the crucial component requiring our brother's repentance in order for him to be freed and restored. The application of forgiveness done within our own heart keeps our heart free from unforgiveness and open to receive forgiveness from God. It does not deliver our brother from his enslavement to sin, his captivity by the devil, or cause us to gain our brother. In order for our brother to be delivered from his enslavement to sin, his captivity by the devil, and restored he must *"...repent..."* for his sin.

Forgiveness without repentance is dead
to accomplish the will of God on our brother's behalf!

THE RIDDLE

Look again at Paul's instructions to Timothy in these matters:

> "...A servant of the Lord must not quarrel but be gentle to all, able to teach, patient, in humility correcting those who are in opposition (...who oppose themselves... KJV), if God perhaps will grant them repentance, so that they may know the truth, and that they may come to their senses and escape the snare of the devil, having been taken captive by him to do his will..."
>
> **II Timothy 2:24-26**

Repentance is necessary for the sinning brother to *"...come to their senses and escape the snare of the devil..."*. Requiring the sinning brother to repent of his sin does not place a heavy burden on him; it is God's means for him to be freed. Unless the sinning brother repents he will remain a slave to sin, a captive of the devil, and have some degree of separation from the church. The sinning brother causes all of these things to happen to himself by his unwillingness to repent. Jesus said,

> "Come to Me, all you who labor and are heavy laden, and I will give you rest. Take My yoke upon you and learn from Me, for I am gentle and lowly in heart, and you will find rest for your souls. For My yoke is easy and My burden is light." **Matthew 11:28-30**

> "I am the way, the truth, and the life..." **John 14:6**

What we learn from Jesus is the way we are designed to live in His church. His way could be called the *"...rules..."* of His House. Because He is the Head of the church, His own House and Body, we are expected to walk by His *"...rules..."*.

However, He can make exceptions to these rules. One such exception regarding going to the sinning brother telling him his fault, receiving his repentance for his sin in order for him to be freed and restored can be seen in Jesus' relationship with Peter.

Just prior to Jesus' crucifixion Peter denied Jesus three times; his denials involved lies and curses. This event holds such significance in the kingdom that all four gospels record accounts of it *(Matthew 26:31-35, 69-75; Mark 14:27-31, 66-72; Luke 22:31-34; and John13:36-38, 15:15-18, 25-27)*. After Jesus was raised from the dead and joined Himself to His disciples, He never mentioned Peter's denials even though Peter clearly violated the will of God in those denials. Instead, He made Peter breakfast on the beach.

Jesus' actions involving Peter are exceptions to Jesus' instructions presented in *Matthew 18:15-17*, *"...if your brother sins against you, go and tell him his fault between you and him alone. If he hears you, you have gained your brother..."*. Jesus' exception creates a precedent we certainly have a right to follow, but we must follow it with great caution. We must make absolutely certain God the Holy Spirit is inspiring the exception, and the brethren who are capable judge the exception to be God's direction regarding the sin a brother has committed against us. It cannot be just a good idea we have conceived from within our own heart or head or what we think is the *"...right..."* thing to do. We do not want to become legalistic in following the *"...rules..."* Jesus gives us, but we equally do not want to cast the rules out on the basis of personal thought. We must constantly remember that Jesus is the one who is supreme in authority over the church and loves us more than anyone else could possibly love us. His care for His own flesh and bone body parts will *"...always..."* be greater than anything we could conceive of doing on their behalf. We simply need to receive, understand, and follow *His* instructions!

Chapter Five

SIN'S FAR REACHING AFFECTS

We have already seen the devastating effects of sin on the individual who sins, but does sin reach beyond the one who sins? We are continually establishing that Jesus' instructions on dealing with the sinning brother are not punitive in nature. Jesus loves the sinning brother, and His instructions on how to deal with him are motivated by His desire to see him freed from enslavement to sin, captivity by the devil, and the measure of death of which he has partaken. These facts are absolute and irrefutable!

Building on the foundation of this absolute and irrefutable knowledge, Jesus has included in His instructions a directive in the event our brother refuses to hear us and repent. We are to treat him, *"...like a heathen and a tax collector..."*. Since there are no specific scripture references describing the treatment of the heathen and the tax collectors per se, perhaps we can simply achieve agreement on Jesus' words that Jesus expects the basis of our relationship with the unrepentant sinning brother to change. Two questions arise from this agreement:

➤ *To what does our relationship change?*

➤ *Why is Jesus requiring a change of relationship?*

Here we must restate once again that Jesus is not declaring a punitive result for the unrepentant brother, nor is His love for our brother threatened, nor is Jesus changing the unrepentant brother's salvation. Jesus loves the flesh of His flesh and bone of His bone parts of His body. He desires for the sinning brother to be freed from his enslavement to sin, his captivity by the devil, and the measure of death of which he has partaken. None of these things have changed! However, it is abundantly clear that Jesus, as supreme in authority over the church, is directing us to change the basis of our relationship with the unrepentant brother!

It is absolutely impossible for a person who sees and thinks like a mere man to understand Jesus' directive. The mere-man-minded person will reason away what Jesus has instructed us to do or will justify why Jesus' love, mercy, and grace would not allow us to follow the instructions Jesus Himself has given. Only a spiritual person can understand and follow Jesus' instructions in faith believing they are full of love, mercy, and grace, and are motivated to heal, deliver, and forgive the unrepentant brother and protect the church.

By inspiration of God the Holy Spirit Paul wrote letters to the church at Thessalonica, at Corinth, and to Titus including instructions similar to those given by Jesus. We gain some insight as to what the change of relationship looks like through the writings of Paul starting with Paul's letter to the church at Thessalonica.

SIN'S AFFECTS

*"We command you, brethren, in the name of our Lord Jesus Christ, that you **withdraw from every brother who walks disorderly and not according to the tradition which he received from us**. For you yourselves know how you ought to follow us, for we were not disorderly among you; nor did we eat anyone's bread free of charge, but worked with labor and toil night and day, that we might not be a burden to any of you, not because we do not have authority, but to make ourselves an example of how you should follow us. For we hear that there are some who walk among you in a disorderly manner, not working at all, but are busybodies. Now those who are such we command and exhort through our Lord Jesus Christ that they work in quietness and eat their own bread. But as for you, brethren, do not grow weary in doing good. And **if anyone does not obey our word in this epistle, note that person and do not keep company with him, that he may be ashamed. Yet do not count him as an enemy, but admonish him as a brother.***"*
II Thessalonians 3:6-15

Paul's instructions, inspired by God the Holy Spirit, are easy to see and easy to understand. However, remember, any instructions that pertain to sin must not be treated whimsically. They cannot stand alone; they must be built on the foundation of what we have already received from the Lord Jesus. We do *"...not..."* withdraw from every brother who walks disorderly, or note the brother who disobeys the word of this epistle, or stop keeping company with him *"...unless..."* we have first gone to our brother and told him his sin giving him a chance to repent and be gained as our brother. Even if our brother refuses to hear and repent after following Jesus' instructions and the instructions written by Paul, we still do *"...not..."* treat our brother as an enemy, but admonish him as a brother. Our ability to admonish him implies some type of involvement with him, but with a distinct change in our relationship with him. Another such instruction written by Paul was written to the church at Corinth.

> *"I wrote to you in my epistle not to keep company with sexually immoral people. Yet I certainly did not mean with the sexually immoral people of this world, or with the covetous, or extortioners, or idolaters, since then you would need to go out of the world. But now **I have written to you not to keep company with anyone named a brother, who is sexually immoral, or covetous, or an idolater, or a reviler, or a drunkard, or an extortioner, not even to eat with such a person.** For what have I to do with judging those also who are outside? Do you not judge those who are inside? But those who are outside God judges. Therefore "**put away from yourselves the evil person.**" I Corinthians 5:9-13*

These instructions must also be founded on Jesus' instructions in order for them to produce Jesus' results. In other words, we do not stop keeping company with any believer as our first step in dealing with the sinning brother. We must first have followed Jesus' instructions and have gone to our brother to tell him his sin giving him a chance to repent and be gained as our brother. If he refuses to hear us and to repent, then we change the basis of our relationship with him and stop keeping company with him.

Paul's letter to Titus also presents clear and understandable instructions regarding changing the basis of our relationship with an unrepentant brother.

> *"**Reject (3868) a divisive man after the first and second admonition,** knowing that such a person is warped and sinning, being self-condemned."* **Titus 3:10**

SIN'S AFFECTS

3868 paraiteomai from *3844* and the mid. of *154*; to
beg off, i.e. *deprecate, decline, shun*: -- avoid, (make)
excuse, intreat, refuse, reject.

The words Paul wrote *"...after the first and second admonition..."* show the love, mercy, grace, and patience the Lord expects us to have in our involvement with a sinning brother before actually *"...rejecting (or ...avoiding...)..."* him.

Paul's writings have shown us that even if the sinning brother does not repent, we are *not* to treat him as an enemy, but rather as a brother. Even though his status as a brother is still in effect, he no longer has access to the benefits of his church family: We do not keep company with him. We do not eat with him. We put him away from ourselves. We avoid him. The illustration of a person who violated the law in the natural world and was separated from his family by the legal system again serves to help our understanding in this matter. Such a person is still loved by his family, still a part of his family, but separated from them. Such a person no longer can enjoy the benefits of his family: No more personal fellowship.

Paul has specifically addressed the sins of *"...walking disorderly, sexual immorality, covetousness, extortion, idolatry, and divisiveness..."* in his letters to the churches at Thessalonica, Corinth, and Titus. There is another subtle device the enemy has used against the church regarding sins: Sins can be ranked as to lesser or greater, and these lesser or greater sins differ in consequences. The enemy would not be able to install his devices unless they were subtle and contained some element of truth, albeit truth corrupted. The consequences of our sins in this natural world may be able to be graded on a continuum, but these natural world consequences are not spirit world oriented. For example, in the natural world the consequence for stealing your neighbor's lawn mower is not as great as for you stealing your neighbor's car. Following the natural world logic would, therefore, make stealing a lawn mower a lesser sin than stealing a car. However, this wisdom does not descend from above but is earthly. Any sin carries the consequence of enslavement to sin and captivity by the devil as we have already seen in Paul's letters to the church at Rome *(Romans 6:16)*, and to Timothy *(II Timothy 2:24-26)*. Changing the basis for relating to the sinning brother is not, however, sin-specific. That is, if our brother sins some particular sin we must change the basis for relating to him. *No!*

> *Changing the basis for relating to the sinning brother is his unwillingness to hear his brother who comes to him to tell him his fault and his unwillingness to repent.*

The change of relationship has a very distinct look:

"...withdraw from the brother..."

"...note that person and do not keep company with him, that he may be ashamed..."

"...put away from yourselves the evil person..."

50

"...do not keep company with the brother...not even to eat with such a person..."

"...reject a divisive man ..."

Yet do not count him as an enemy, but admonish him as a brother!

Now, why is Jesus requiring such changes of relationship with the unrepentant brother? We must find an appropriate and accurate answer to this question in order to be able to anchor our faith properly. Because the enemy has made the revelation of sin, forgiveness, and repentance a riddle we must be very careful in our efforts to *"...restore..."* the way of the Lord back into the church. The restoration must be full of simplicity, an easy yoke, and a light burden or the church will not embrace it.

We must restate our understanding of Jesus here. Jesus is full of love, mercy, and grace! The prophet Jeremiah recorded the Lord speaking about Himself. Jeremiah wrote,

> *"For I know the thoughts that I think toward you, says the Lord, thoughts of peace and not of evil, to give you a future and a hope." **Jeremiah 29:11***

Absolutely nothing Jesus wills for us is harmful against us. We are His own flesh and bone body. His will for the manner in which we deal with our sinning brother is not punitive against our brother. His will is the *"...means..."* to help our

51

brother be freed from his enslavement to sin, his captivity by the devil, and the measure of death of which he has partaken. His will is to protect the church. *His will is yes, and amen!!!* We are laboring to present truth in these matters in such a way so that we may walk in the truth which has been stolen from us and to identify and remove the corruption the enemy has used against us.

We turn again to the writings of Paul as he writes to the troubled church at Corinth. The church at Corinth were suffering from sexual immorality in their midst but were not dealing with it. In Paul's letter to them he gave them a serious rebuke for not dealing with the sin and instructions on how to deal with it. In the last portion of Paul's instructions he presented them with wisdom regarding the *"...reason..."* they needed to deal with the sin in their midst. He wrote...

> *"Do you now know that **a little leaven leavens the whole lump**? Therefore purge out the old leaven, that you may be a new lump, since you truly are unleavened. For indeed Christ, our Passover, was sacrificed for us. Therefore let us keep the feast, not with old leaven, nor with the leaven of malice and wickedness, but with the unleavened bread of sincerity and truth."*
>
> ***I Corinthians 5:6,8***

Paul likens *"...sin..."* to *"...leaven..."*. The concept, that a *"...little leaven leavens the whole lump..."* from the natural world, is not a difficult concept to understand. Even if it takes a small demonstration, we can illustrate the effects of only a little leaven on a lump of bread dough. It is stunning!!!

The *"...leaven..."* analogy is easy enough to leverage from the natural world to its application in the spirit. Whatever sin is committed, it will act like *"...leaven..."* and have an **incredible impact** on the whole church, just like natural *"...leaven..."* has an **incredible impact** on the whole lump even though only a tiny amount is sown into the lump.

Life is lived out of the abundance of the heart for both the saved and the unsaved man. Jesus taught this simple truth in various encounters He had with both disciples and the Pharisees. He spoke to the disciples in the sermon on the mount as recorded in Matthew the sixth chapter, and then, to the Pharisees in the twelfth chapter.

> *"Do not lay up for yourselves treasures on earth, where moth and rust destroy and where thieves break in and steal; but lay up for yourselves treasures in heaven, where neither moth nor rust destroys and where thieves do not break in and steal. For **where your treasure is, there your heart will be also.**" **Matthew 6:19-21***

> *"**No one can serve two masters**; for either he will hate the one and love the other, or else he will be loyal to the one and despise the other. You cannot serve God and mammon." **Matthew 6:24***

> *"Either make the tree good and its fruit good, or else make the tree bad and its fruit bad; for a tree is known by its fruit. Brood of vipers! How can you, being evil, speak good things? For **out of the abundance of the heart the mouth speaks.** A good man out of the good treasure of his heart brings forth good things, and an evil man out of the evil treasure brings forth evil things."* ***Matthew 12:33-37***

An unrepentant brother is unrepentant out of the abundance of his heart. The unrepentant brother sinned out of the abundance of his heart. The unrepentant brother, as do all of us, lives out of the abundance of his heart. The unrepentant brother sinned because he shifted his view of life from spiritually minded to carnally minded. Spiritually minded is life and peace; carnally minded is death.

Jesus wills for us to go to our brother who has sinned against us to tell him his sin, yes, but at a deeper level He desires for the sinning brother to see he has chosen carnally minded so he can shift back to spiritually minded. The church at Corinth serves to illustrate this very principle. Paul told them they were full of envy, strife, and divisions, all of which were violations of the Lord's will. However, Paul used these sins as symptoms to identify their carnal condition. Paul was endeavoring to get them back to spiritual mindedness.

> *"And I, brethren, could not speak to you as to spiritual people but as to carnal, as to babes in Christ. I fed you with milk and not with solid food; for until now you were not able to receive it, and even now you are still not able; for you are still carnal. For where there are envy, strife, and divisions among you, are you not carnal and behaving like mere men?"* **I Corinthians 3:1-3**

This shift from spiritually minded to carnally minded is a change of heart. This change of heart does not mean the sinning believer is no longer saved. It simply means the sinning believer has chosen to be after the things of the flesh instead of the things of the spirit; something we could all do.

SIN'S AFFECTS

Jesus addressed this matter in His words regarding the difference in perspectives regarding *"...adultery..."* between the old covenant and the new covenant.

*"You have heard that it was said to those of old, 'You shall not commit adultery.' But I say to you that who-ever looks at a woman to lust for her **has already committed adultery with her in his heart.**" Matthew 5:27,28*

We could say, according to the words of Jesus Himself, that the born again person who committed adultery did so out of the abundance of his heart. I am confident no one would contend that a person who is born again could *not* commit adultery. I am equally confident that no one would contend that if a born again person did commit adultery, they did so as a spiritually minded person.

The born again person who committed the sin of adultery could only have done so because he was *"...drawn away by his own desires and enticed..."* (See **James 1:12-16, esp 13 & 14**). Being drawn away by your own desires are directly related to the desires of your flesh. Paul wrote to the church at Rome that...

*"...those who live according to the flesh set their minds on the things of the flesh, but those who live according to the spirit, the things of the spirit. For to be carnally minded is death, but to be spiritually minded is life and peace. Because the carnal mind is enmity against God; for it is not subject to the law of God, nor indeed can be..." **Romans 8:5-8***

THE RIDDLE

The only way it is possible for a born again believer to sin after they have chosen spiritually minded as a way of life is if they shift from spiritually minded to carnally minded. The cause for such a shift would be directly related to the desires of their flesh. The moment their flesh desired a thing that was a clear violation of the will of God, and such a person began to think on the desire of their flesh in a wanton fashion, sin occurred in their heart. Out of the abundance of their heart carnal mindedness and sin will then emerge as the practice of their life.

The changes of relationship Jesus is requiring of us are for at least two reasons: So that the unrepentant brother may be ashamed, hopefully stimulating him to see the error of his life; and so that the unrepentant sin of our brother will not act like leaven to the rest of our lives. *Sin has far reaching affects!*

Chapter Six

DIVINELY EMPOWERED PROVISIONS

Every component of the new covenant is God's provision based on the death, burial, and resurrection of the Christ. Paul wrote to the church at Corinth explaining the stark contrasts between the old covenant and the new covenant. He used his own life to illustrate how living under the old covenant, endeavoring to fulfill what he knew to be the will of God in his own power, only produced failure and hopelessness. Paul's explanation of the transition from life lived under the old covenant back to life available in the new covenant is very poignant.

> *"O wretched man that I am! Who will deliver me from this body of death? I thank God through Jesus Christ our Lord! So then, with the mind I myself serve the law of God, but with the flesh the law of sin. There is therefore now no condemnation to those who are in Christ Jesus, who do not walk according to the flesh, but according to the spirit. For the law of the Spirit of life in Christ Jesus has made me free from the law of sin and death..."* **Romans 7:24 -8:2**

When Paul writes *"...with the mind I myself serve the law of God, but with the flesh the law of sin..."* he is not committing us to sin nor excusing us from sin because of the weakness of our flesh. He is simply expressing his understanding that even though we have been born again, our flesh has not yet been glorified. Our unglorified flesh has desires that if allowed to conceive will produce sin. We have already seen Jesus' flesh had desires at the end of His forty day fast yet He remained without sin. James gives us a simple, clear, and understandable God-inspired revelation on this particular matter:

> *"Blessed is the man who endures temptation; for when he has been approved, he will receive the crown of life which the Lord has promised to those who love Him. Let no one say when he is tempted, "I am tempted by God"; for God cannot be tempted by evil, not does He Himself tempt anyone. But each one is tempted when he is drawn away by his own desires and enticed. Then, when desire has conceived, it gives birth to sin; and sin, when it is full-grown, brings forth death..."*
>
> ***James 1:12-15***

When Luke wrote about Jesus' journey *"...into the wilderness being tempted forty days by the devil..."* he was showing us that Jesus' flesh was made just like ours: ***...able to be tempted!*** Luke wrote at the end of Jesus' forty day fast He was *"...hungry..."*. Hunger was the desire of Jesus' flesh to eat what had been forbidden while He was fasting. Jesus' flesh desiring bread was what made Satan's proposal of turning the stone into bread a temptation. According to the understanding given to us by James the desire of Jesus' flesh was not sin because Jesus did not give Himself to consider the desire of His flesh in a wanton manner. No sin occurred, although His flesh desired a thing forbidden.

PROVISIONS

Until it is time in the new covenant for believers to receive glorified new flesh, our unglorified flesh is going to desire things that will tempt us. Paul, once again, provides us with revelation to show us how to overcome the desires of our flesh.

> *"Walk in the spirit, and you shall not fulfill the lust of the flesh. For the flesh lusts against the spirit, and the spirit against the flesh; and these are contrary to one another, so that you do not do the things that you wish. But if you are led by the Spirit, you are not under the law. Now the works of the flesh are evident, which are: adultery, fornication, uncleanness, lewdness, idolatry, sorcery, hatred, contentions, jealousies, outbursts of wrath, selfish ambitions, dissensions, heresies, envy, murders, drunkenness, revelries, and the like..."*
> **Galatians 5:16-21**

The ability the born again new creature has to *"...walk in the spirit..."* so as not to fulfill *"...the lust of the flesh..."* is a divinely empowered provision from God. This provision is called *"...faith..."*!

The apostles came to Jesus asking Him to increase their faith. Jesus replied,

> *"If you have faith as a mustard seed, you can say to this mulberry tree, 'Be pulled up by the roots and be planted in the sea.' and it would obey you."*...**Luke 17:6**

In other similar scripture references Jesus spoke of *"...casting mountains into the sea..."* and *"...nothing being impossible..."* if done in faith. We can surely see a provision no larger than a mustard seed capable of moving trees and mountains into the sea is not of this world. God has provided us with faith as His gift to us so that we may be able to live successfully in His kingdom and to do His whole will for our lives.

Even though we have God's provisions to help us walk in the spirit and not fulfill the lusts of our flesh, we still have the potential to sin. Adam was made like God to be able to rule over all the works of God's hands but still had the potential to sin. God gave Adam free will to obey Him or not to obey Him, just like He does us in the new covenant. In the event that a born again new creature in Christ chooses carnal minded over spiritual minded and sins, God has made provision for such a new creature to recover from his sin. John wrote in his first epistle...

> *"My little children, these things I write to you, so that you may not sin. And if anyone sins, we have an Advocate with the Father, Jesus Christ the righteous. And He Himself is the propitiation for our sins, and not for ours only but also for the whole world."* **I John 2:1,2**

When Jesus gave instructions regarding how to deal with a sinning brother, He used the term *"...brother..."* signifying a member of the household of God was able to sin. The divinely empowered provisions God has given us to be able to deal with sin are *"...forgiveness..."* and *"...repentance..."*. Both of these have natural world counterparts, but the forgiveness and repentance of the new covenant are based on the death, burial, and resurrection of Christ, therefore markedly different from forgiveness and repentance of the natural world.

PROVISIONS

God's provisions for us to be able to deal with sin operating through Christ as the sacrifice for our sins is a completely new type of sacrifice: *Christ does not cover sin; He takes sin away.* While baptizing people in the wilderness John the Baptist saw Jesus coming toward him and said,

> *"Behold! The Lamb of God who takes away the sin of the world!"* **John 1:29**

Many Jewish believers were falling away from Christ as a result of persecution from fellow Jews who had rejected Christ as the way. The writer of the letter to the Hebrew Christians labored carefully to establish the need for Christ and for the new covenant on behalf of these Jewish believers who were falling away. Much the writer's letter revolved around the need for a new type of sacrifice for sins as seen summarized in these following few verses:

> *"...the law, having a shadow of the good things to come, and not the very image of the things, can never with these same sacrifices, which they offer continually year by year, make those who approach perfect (5048). For then would they not have ceased to be offered? For the worshippers, once purified, would have had no more consciousness of sins. But in those sacrifices there is a reminder of sins every year. For it is not possible that the blood of bulls and goats could take away sins."*
> ***Hebrews 10:1-4***

5048 teleioo from *5046*; to *complete*, i.e. (lit.) *accomplish*, or (fig.) *consummate* (in character): -- consecrate, finish, fulfill, (make) perfect.

THE RIDDLE

Under the old covenant sins were merely covered, not taken away leaving those who sinned having to deal with sin year after year. When the fullness of time came, Jesus entered as God's provision to *"...take sin away..."*, not just provide another sacrificial covering for sin.

What about Christ allowed Him to *"...take sin away..."?* The answer comes as a revelation comprised of two parts. The first part deals with Jesus walking on earth as a man. In letters written to the church at Rome, Corinth, Philippi, and to the Hebrew Christians we find the first part of this revelation.

> *"For the law of the Spirit of life in Christ Jesus has made me free from the law of sin and death.* ***For what the law could not do in that it was weak through the flesh, God did by sending His own Son in the likeness of sinful flesh, on account of sin: He condemned sin in the flesh,*** *that the righteous requirement of the law might be fulfilled in us who do not walk according to the flesh but according to the Spirit."* ***Romans 8:2-4***

Jesus came into this world born of a virgin so the sin of the man Adam did not pass into him. Although born sinless, Jesus still had to live free of sin on the earth as a man. Yes, He remained God because whatever kind of seed you plant, that is what will be produced. God's seed was planted; God was produced. However, by divine design, Jesus divested Himself of His divine attributes to live on the earth as a man so that as the Last Adam he could provide redemption for all mankind who had partaken of the First Adam's sin.

PROVISIONS

"For since by man came death, by Man also came the resurrection of the dead. for as in Adam all die, even so in Christ all shall be made alive..."

I Corinthians 15:21,22

Adam yielded to sin while living on earth as a *"...man..."*, so another *"...man..."* must overcome sin while living on the earth. Jesus' humble willingness to live on earth as a man allowing Himself to be made *"...in all ways like His brethren..."*, but still overcome sin while He walked as a man, created the way for Him to provide salvation for all who would believe. This is the first part of the revelation explaining how Jesus could *"...take sin away..."*.

"...Inasmuch then as the children have partaken of flesh and blood, He Himself likewise shared in the same, that through death He might destroy him who had the power of death, that is, the devil, and release those who through fear of death were all their lifetime subject to bondage. For indeed He does not give aid to angels, but He does give aid to the seed of Abraham. Therefore, in all things He had to be made like His brethren, that He might be a merciful and faithful High Priest in things pertaining to God, to make propitiation for the sins of the people. For in that He Himself has suffered, being tempted, He is able to aid those who are tempted." Hebrews 2:14-18

"Let this mind be in you which was also in Christ Jesus, who, being in the form of God, did not consider it robbery to be equal with God, but made Himself of no reputation, taking the form of a bond-servant, and coming in the likeness of men. And being found in appearance as a man, He humbled Himself and became obedient to the point of death, even the death of the cross. Therefore God also has highly exalted Him and given Him the name which is above every name, that at the name

of Jesus every knee should bow, of those in heaven, and of those on earth, and of those under the earth, and that every tongue should confess that Jesus Christ is Lord, to the glory of God the Father." **Philippians 2:5-11**

Jesus' assignment on earth not only required Him to live as a man free of sin for his own personal life but also to be willing to die as the penalty for the sins of all mankind. Upon completion of His earthly tasks God the Father raised Him from the dead and exalted Him giving Him the name which is above every name: **Lord!** Mankind's access to Jesus as the new type of sacrifice that takes our sin away is predicated on the revelation that Jesus is Lord! Salvation is through Lordship!

"...If you confess with your mouth the Lord Jesus and believe in your heart that God has raised Him from the dead, you will be saved. For with the heart one believes unto righteousness, and with the mouth confession is made unto salvation..." **Romans 10:9,10**

The second part of the mystery regarding Christ taking away sin rather than just covering it, deals with God's strategic design of salvation for all who believe. The moment a person believes and is born again, they are baptized into Christ to become a flesh and bone part of His body. This act of baptism into Christ causes us to be identified with Christ in His death, His burial, and His resurrection.

*"What shall we say then? Shall we continue in sin that grace may abound? Certainly not! How shall we who died to sin live any longer in it? Or **do you not know that as many of us as were baptized into Christ Jesus were baptized into His death?** Therefore we were buried with Him through baptism into death, that just as*

Christ was raised from the dead by the glory of the Father, even so we also should walk in newness of life. For *if we have been united together in the likeness of His death, certainly we also shall be in the likeness of His resurrection, knowing this, that **our old man was crucified with Him, that the body of sin might be done away with, that we should no longer be slaves of sin. For he who has died has been freed from sin...***"

Romans 6:1-6

When God the Father looks at us individually in Christ, He sees us crucified just as He sees Christ crucified. He sees our old body of sin as dead. He sees us resurrected and alive as flesh and bone parts of Christ. God's strategic plan for salvation caused us to be identified with Christ in such a way that we actually partook of Jesus' death as if we ourselves had died.

"He who has died has been freed from sin!"

In this way, Jesus took away sins, not just covered them. A person who has died has no more consciousness of sin. He has no more sin. God's new covenant forgiveness is based on Jesus' death, and our death, too. We have died and are freed from sin!

With this understanding of new covenant forgiveness we must consider *"...repentance..."* in new covenant terms. ***Strong's Exhaustive Concordance of the Bible*** lists the English term *"...repentance..."* as number *3341*, identifying the Greek term *"...metanoia..."*.

3341 metanoia from *3340*; (subj.) *compunction* (for guilt, includ. *reformation*); by impl. *reversal* (of [another's] decision): -- repentance.

The natural world counterpart of new covenant *"...repentance..."* is defined as:

> the act of repenting or the state of being penitent; sorrow or regret for what has been done or left undone by oneself; especially, sorrow and contrition for sin; such sorrow for the past as leads to amendment of one's ways; penitence; contrition.

> **Webster's New Universal Unabridged Dictionary**

The natural world definition of repentance is basically sorrow for past actions or inactions. However, scripture distinguishes between godly sorrow and the sorrow of the world.

> *"For godly sorrow produces repentance leading to salvation, not to be regretted; but the sorrow of the world produces death."* **II Corinthians 7:10**

If a person equates sorrow with new covenant repentance, such a person will fall short of God's provision. Sorrow is merely the first step toward repentance. New covenant repentance leads a person to salvation, salvation from enslavement to sin and captivity of the devil by which a person has been bound through sin.

Revisiting James' writings regarding the manner in which a person enters into sin will be profitable here. James wrote...

> *"Let no one say when he is tempted, "I am tempted by God"; for God cannot be tempted by evil, nor does He*

Himself tempt anyone. But each one is tempted when he is drawn away by his own desires and enticed. Then, when desire has conceived, it gives birth to sin; and sin, when it is full-grown, brings forth death."

James 1:13-15

A believer does not enter directly into sin. He is tempted to sin when he is drawn away by his own desires and enticed. Then when desire has conceived, it gives birth to sin; and sin, when it is full-grown, brings forth death.

Looking at the *"...process..."* that leads to sin will be extremely helpful here. A born again believer has been baptized into Christ, including His death, burial, and resurrection. Such a believer is dead to sin and freed from the power of it. His flesh has not yet been glorified so it still must be ruled by the believer's spirit using the divinely empowered gift God has given him, faith. The only way this gift will work is if the born again person is spiritual. That is, the person is after the things of the spirit rather than the things of the flesh.

Throughout the course of time the flesh will desire things that are not within the scope of God's will. Paul gives us a list *(not meant to be exhaustive)* of the works of the flesh that are not according to God's will: *"...adultery, fornication, uncleanness, lewdness, idolatry, sorcery, hatred, contentions, jealousies, outbursts of wrath, selfish ambitions, dissensions, heresies, envy, murders, drunkenness, revelries, and the like...".* The more mature a believer is the more skilled he will be at ruling over his flesh and resisting its desires. This is not a sin-free card for immature and unskilled believers! It is merely an accurate understanding of the growth process...

A babe-in-Christ provides us with an illustration easy to see. Suppose he is peacefully and legally driving down the road when suddenly approached from behind by a speeding vehicle that passes him on a double yellow line. The babe-in-Christ is neither mature nor skilled in walking out his salvation by faith in fear and trembling. Such a babe-in-Christ has a greater potential to yield to the desires of his flesh than does a more mature believer who better understands the consequences of sin and is more skilled in the means to overcome the desires of his flesh. The babe-in-Christ, without much thought or application of faith, yields to the desires of his flesh and *"...bursts out in wrath..."* aimed at the foolish driver passing him on the double yellow line. His actions are a violation of the will of God. They are sin.

Is the sin and its consequence complete when the outburst of wrath is over? ...or once the babe-in-Christ settles his emotions after a little time has passed? After all the babe-in-Christ is immature and unskilled; he couldn't help himself. Besides all that, it is not really his fault; that foolish driver shouldn't have passed him on a double yellow line. And anyway, everyone loses his cool ever now and then. God knows the babe-in-Christ's heart... *Is this the pattern for dealing with sin:* **Time heals all?**

No one, absolutely no one, can change the consequences for sin. Enslavement to sin, captivity by the devil, and partaking of a measure of death are not results of a greater sin and yet not applicable to the lesser sin. This is the corruption from the enemy. Whosoever yields himself to sin that one becomes a slave to the sin to whom he yields himself. This revelation is not intended to make everyone feel hopeless regarding sin, on the contrary. This revelation is intended to present the destructive nature of sin and to release the fear of the Lord among us so that we may avoid sin. Jesus does not hate those who sin; He hates sin. He was willing to die to redeem us from the power of sin. Why would He not reveal to us from what He has redeemed us?

Look again at the illustration of the babe-in-Christ bursting out in wrath while driving. Add these ingredients to this illustration. The wrathful babe-in-Christ has passengers, his wife and two young children. The consequence of the sin will not be contained to just the one who sinned. The man's wife will most likely be embarrassed. The man's children have just been given a pattern for dealing with the issues of life. Now the children believe outbursts of wrath are perfectly acceptable as the means of dealing with certain issues in life.

Even if the babe-in-Christ burst out in wrath in the presence of his family, God could have made his actions work together for his good. Instead of justifying the outburst, the man could have yielded to the convicting ministry of the Holy Spirit seeing his actions from God's perspective. If the sinning man would have acknowledged his actions as sin, divinely empowered provisions would have been set in motion: firstly, causing the man to repent of his sin, stopping the power of his sin from ruling over him; secondly, it would have caused the man to see the need to receive forgiveness by faith from God to take his sin away, not merely cover it; and thirdly, it would have presented the correct model of behavior for the man's family. This model for dealing with sin is the design of the Lord!

However, the design of the Lord is not currently in operation regarding sin, forgiveness, and repentance in the church. There is a corrupt model in its place. The corrupt model is established in the church not because the sons of God love evil and refuse to stop sinning. The corrupt model is established in the church through the subtle craftiness of the enemy who has labored diligently and patiently for generations to corrupt our knowledge of sin, forgiveness, and repentance. He has made them a riddle! Now is the time to identify the dark corruption of his work by revealing the truth!

Once the truth is available to us, then we must decide whether or not we will embrace the truth or continue to walk out the corrupt model. After we know the truth if we choose the corrupt model, it will be because we would rather have free access to sin as the enemy has convinced us: *"Everyone sins; it is just impossible not to sin, but God knows our heart!"* God does know our heart, but it is a lie to say it is just impossible not to sin!

We must choose "...a lie..." or "...the truth..."!!!

SUMMARY & CONCLUSION

The revelation of sin, forgiveness, and repentance were never intended to be *"...riddles...*"! Understanding for each of these three is compulsory if we, as the people of God, are ever going to live successfully here on earth. We must know the truth God the Holy Spirit desires to give us regarding each of these, which will in turn expose the corruption of the enemy leaving us two options, to continue in the *"...lie..."* or embrace the *"...truth...".*

The church, the sons of God, born again new creatures in Christ in massive numbers believe it is impossible to overcome *"...sin...*"! Many of this same number further believe that God understands the difficulty in trying to overcome sin, and He makes allowances because He knows the heart. Jesus, as the Lamb of God sent to take away the sin of the world, fulfilled His mission, and is now the means for us to be able to deal with sin, and yet the church, His flesh and bone body parts believe it is just too hard to overcome sin.

The church has been deceived!

Webster's New Universal Unabridged Dictionary defines *"...deceived..."* as...

...to make a person believe what is not true; to mislead; to cause to err; to delude; to cheat; to beguile.

Oh, the horror of sin! *"**Sin** was the reason..."* Adam lost his place in God, was stripped of his authority, was expelled from the garden, and died. Sin enslaves those who sin, captures men for the devil, and has as its wages death.

Is there any way out?

Yes, thank God, He has made a way!

He sent His only begotten son into the earth to die as the means to take away the sin of the world. Embracing the truth will, however, require an enormous amount of change in our individual and our corporate lives, change only possible in the power of God. Abba has designed the church to live in His power! It is up to us to allow Him to show us we have already partaken of His power. We just need to learn how to *"...use..."* it to make the changes He is requiring of us.

We can do this!

www.ingramcontent.com/pod-product-compliance
Lightning Source LLC
Chambersburg PA
CBHW071841020426
42331CB00007B/1810